MW01141328

Presented to

_____

By

_____

On

_____

Other Books You Will Want to Read:

International Children's Bible
Every Day With God
My Little Bible
International Children's Story Bible
Amy Grant's Heart-to-Heart Bible Stories
What Does God Do?

The
Bible
for Beginning
Readers

WORD PUBLISHING
Dallas·London·Vancouver·Melbourne

THE BIBLE FOR BEGINNING READERS:
Favorite Stories from the text of the *International Children's Bible*

Library of Congress Cataloging-in-Publication Data:

Bible. English. International Children's Bible. Selections. 1991.
    The Bible for beginning readers : favorite stories from the text of the International Children's Bible.
       p. cm.
    Summary: A collection of Bible stories, psalms, and proverbs from the International Children's Bible.
    ISBN 0–8499–0917–1
    I. Word Publishing. II. Title.
BS391.2 1991
220.5'208—dc20   91–30792
                                        CIP
                                        AC

1 2 3 4 9 AGH 9 8 7 6 5 4 3 2 1

Printed in the United States of America

Dear Parent:

Caution! This book is extremely "child-friendly" and may cause addiction to God's Word!

The Bible for Beginning Readers contains stories from the Old and New Testaments—stories of heroes and sinners, God's miracles and grace, and the person of Jesus Christ—all presented in a simple, yet accurate, format. It is colorfully illustrated and easy to read.

The stories are taken from the *International Children's Bible,* a translation just for kids, developed by twenty-one scholars over many years. It was tested and proven to be the *most readable translation* for children.

You as a parent can trust it for accuracy, yet your children can read it on their own. You will love these Bible stories for your children—if they ever give you a turn to read it.

The Publisher

Contents

Old Testament Stories
and Selected Psalms and Proverbs

New Testament Stories
and Selected Psalms and Proverbs

New Testament (cont.)

Old Testament Stories

and selected

Psalms
and
Proverbs

Genesis 1, 2

God Creates the World

In the beginning God created the sky and the earth. ³Then God said, "Let there be light!" And there was light. ⁵God named the light "day" and the darkness "night." This was the first day.

⁷God made the air to divide the water in two. Some of the water was above the air, and some of the water was below it. ⁸God named the air "sky." This was the second day.

¹⁰God named the dry land "earth." He named the water that was gathered together "seas." God saw that this was good.

¹¹Then God said, "Let the earth produce plants. Every seed will produce more of its own kind of plant." ¹³This was the third day.

[14]Then God said, "Let there be lights in the sky to separate day from night."

[16]So God made the two large lights. He made the brighter light to rule the day. He made the smaller light to rule the night. He also made the stars. [19]This was the fourth day.

[20]Then God said, "Let the water be filled with living things. And let birds fly in the air above the earth." [23]This was the fifth day.

[24]Then God said, "Let the earth be filled with animals. And let each produce more of its own kind. Let there be tame animals and small crawling animals and wild animals." And it happened.

[25]God saw that this was good.

[27]God created human beings in his image. He created them male and female. [28]God blessed them and said, "Have many children and grow in number.

Fill the earth and be its master. Rule over the fish in the sea and over the birds in the sky. Rule over every living thing that moves on the earth."

³¹This was the sixth day.

²:¹The sky, the earth and all that filled them were finished. ²So on the seventh day he rested from all his work. ³God blessed the seventh day and made it a holy day.

The Snake's Trick

The Lord God planted a garden in the East, in a place called Eden. He put the man he had formed in that garden. ⁹God caused every beautiful tree and every tree that was good for food to grow out of the ground. In the middle of the garden God put the tree that gives life, and the tree that gives the knowledge of good and evil.

¹⁵God put the man in the garden to care for it and work it. ¹⁶God commanded him, "Eat the fruit from any tree in the garden. ¹⁷But you must not eat the fruit from the tree which gives the knowledge of good and evil. If you eat fruit from that tree, you will die!"

¹⁸Then God said, "It is not good for the man to be alone. I will make a helper who is right for him."

²²God used the rib from the man to make a woman.

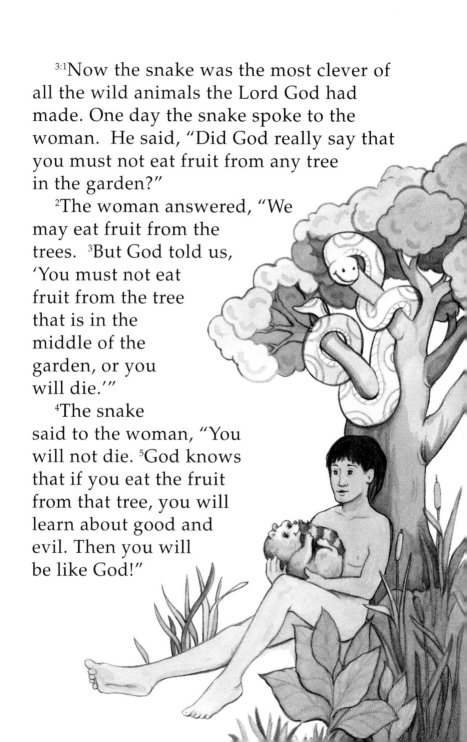

³ː¹Now the snake was the most clever of all the wild animals the Lord God had made. One day the snake spoke to the woman. He said, "Did God really say that you must not eat fruit from any tree in the garden?"

²The woman answered, "We may eat fruit from the trees. ³But God told us, 'You must not eat fruit from the tree that is in the middle of the garden, or you will die.'"

⁴The snake said to the woman, "You will not die. ⁵God knows that if you eat the fruit from that tree, you will learn about good and evil. Then you will be like God!"

⁶So she took some of its fruit and ate it. She also gave some to her husband, and he ate it. ⁷Then, it was as if the man's and the woman's eyes were opened. They realized they were naked. So they made something to cover themselves. ⁸Then they heard the Lord God walking in the garden. ⁹God called to the man. "Where are you?"

[10]The man answered, "I heard you walking in the garden. I was afraid because I was naked. So I hid."

[11]God said, "Who told you that you were naked? Did you eat fruit from that tree?"

[12]The man said, "You gave this woman to me. She gave me fruit from the tree. So I ate it."

[13]God said to the woman, "What have you done?"

She answered, "The snake tricked me. So I ate the fruit."

[14]God said to the snake, "Because you did this, a curse will be put on you. You will crawl on your stomach, and you will eat dust all the days of your life."

¹⁷God said to the man, "You ate fruit from the tree that I commanded you not to eat from.

"So I will put a curse on the ground. You will have to work very hard for food. ¹⁸The ground will produce thorns and weeds for you. ¹⁹You will sweat and work hard. And when you die, you will return to the dust."

²⁰The man named his wife Eve. This is because she is the mother of everyone who ever lived.

²¹The Lord God made clothes from animal skins for the man and his wife. ²²Then God said, "The man knows good and evil. We must keep him from eating some of the fruit from the tree of life. If he does, he will live forever." ²³So the Lord God forced the man out of the garden of Eden.

Noah's Adventure

Noah was a good man. He walked with God. ¹⁰Noah had three sons: Shem, Ham and Japheth.

¹¹People on earth did what God said was evil. ¹²And God saw this evil. ¹³So God said to Noah, "People have made the earth full of violence. So I will destroy all people from the earth. ¹⁴Build a boat of cypress wood for yourself. Make rooms in it and cover it inside and outside with tar. ¹⁶Make an opening around the top of the boat. Put a door in the side of the boat. Make an upper, middle and lower deck in it.

¹⁷I will bring a flood of water on the earth. Everything on the earth will die. ¹⁸But I will make an agreement with you. You, your sons, your wife and your sons' wives will all go into the boat.

¹⁹Also, you must bring into the boat two of every living thing, male and female. Keep them alive with you. ²¹Gather some of every kind of food. Store it on the boat as food for you and the animals."

²²Noah did everything that God commanded him.

⁷ˑ¹Then the Lord said to Noah, ⁴"Seven days from now I will send rain on the earth. It will rain 40 days and 40 nights."

¹¹That day the
underground springs
split open. And the clouds
in the sky poured out rain.
¹³On that same day Noah
and his wife, his sons Shem, Ham
and Japheth and their wives went
into the boat. ¹⁴They had every kind
of wild animal and tame animal.
¹⁶One male and one female of every
living thing came. It was just as
God commanded Noah. Then
the Lord closed the door
behind them.

²¹All living things that moved on the earth died. ²³All that was left was Noah and what was with him in the boat. ²⁴And the waters continued to cover the earth for 150 days.

8:1But God remembered Noah and all the wild animals and tame animals with him in the boat. God made a wind blow over the earth. And the water went down. 2The underground springs stopped flowing. And the clouds in the sky stopped pouring down rain.

*L*ord, tell me your ways.
Show me how to live.

Psalm 25:4

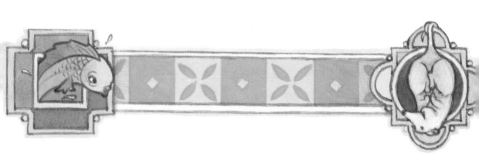

My child, listen to your father's teaching.
And do not forget your mother's advice.

Their teaching will beautify your life.
It will be like flowers in your hair or a chain around your neck.

Proverbs 1:8, 9

Joseph in the Well

Joseph was 17 years old. He and his brothers cared for the flocks. Joseph gave his father bad reports about his brothers.
³Joseph was born when his father, Jacob, was old. He made Joseph a special robe with long sleeves.
⁴Joseph's brothers saw that their father loved Joseph more than he loved them. So they hated their brother.
⁵One time Joseph had a dream. When he told his brothers about it,

they hated him even more. ⁶Joseph said, "Listen to the dream I had. ⁷We were in the field tying bundles of wheat together. My bundle stood up, and your bundles of wheat gathered around mine. Your bundles bowed down to mine."

⁸His brothers said, "Do you really think you will be king over us? Do you truly think you will rule over us?"

⁹Joseph had another dream. He said, "I saw the sun, moon and 11 stars bowing down to me."

¹⁰His father scolded him, saying, "What kind of dream is this? Do you really believe that your mother, your brothers and I will bow down to you?" ¹¹Joseph's brothers were jealous of him. His father thought about what all these things could mean.

¹²One day Joseph's brothers went to herd their father's sheep. ¹⁴His father said, "Go and see if your brothers and the sheep are all right."

¹⁷Joseph went to look for his brothers and found them in Dothan.

¹⁸Joseph's brothers saw him coming from far away. ¹⁹They said, "Here comes that dreamer. ²⁰Let's kill him and throw his

body into one of the wells. We can tell our father that a wild animal killed him."

[21]Reuben said, "Let's not kill him. Throw him into this well here in the desert."
[23]When Joseph came to his brothers, they pulled off his robe. [24]Then they threw him into the well. There was no water in it.

[25]While Joseph was in the well, the brothers sat down to eat.

[26]Judah said to his brothers, "What will we gain if we kill our brother and hide his death? [27]Let's sell him." The other brothers agreed. [28]When traders came by, the brothers took Joseph out of the well. They sold him for eight ounces of silver. And the Ishmaelites took him to Egypt.

[31]The brothers killed a goat and dipped Joseph's long-sleeved robe in its blood. [32]Then they brought the robe to their father. They said, "We found this robe. See if it is your son's robe."

[33]Jacob looked it over and said, "It is my son's robe! Some savage animal has eaten him. My son Joseph has been torn to pieces!" [34]He continued to be sad about his son for a long time.

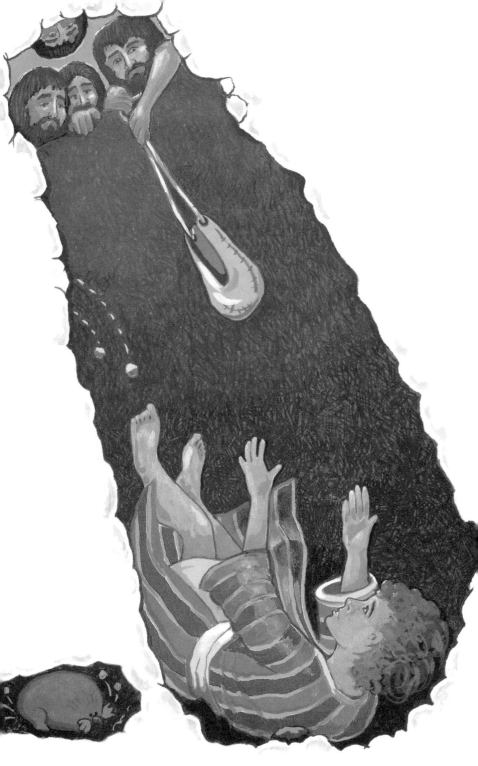

Joseph Rules Egypt

Now Joseph had been taken down to Egypt. ⁴¹:¹⁴The king called for Joseph. ¹⁵The king said, "I have had a dream. But no one can explain its meaning to me."

¹⁶Joseph said, "I am not able to explain dreams. God will do this.

²⁹"You will have seven years of good crops in Egypt. ³⁰But after those seven years, there will come seven years of hunger."

³⁹The king said to Joseph, "God has shown you all this. ⁴⁰I will put you in charge of my palace. All the people will obey your orders."

⁴⁶Joseph was 30 years old when he began serving the king of Egypt. ⁴⁸Joseph gathered all the food which was produced in Egypt during those seven years of good crops. In every city he stored grain that had been grown in the fields around that

city. ^{49}He stored so much grain that he could not measure it.

^{54}Then the seven years of hunger began, just as Joseph had said. In all the lands people had nothing to eat. But in Egypt there was food.

^{57}All the people in that part of the world came to Joseph in Egypt to buy grain.

$^{42:3}$Ten of Joseph's brothers went to buy grain from Egypt. ^{6}So Joseph's brothers came to him.

$^{45:4}$Joseph said to them, "Come close to me. I am your brother Joseph. You sold me as a slave to go to Egypt. ^{5}Now don't be worried. God sent me here ahead of you to save people's lives.

8God has made me the highest officer of the king of Egypt. I am in charge of his palace. I am the master of all the land of Egypt.

9"Leave quickly and go tell my father."

25So the brothers left Egypt and went to their father Jacob. 26They told him, "Joseph is still alive. He is the ruler over all the land of Egypt."

27Now Jacob felt better. 28"My son is alive! I will go and see him."

46:6So Jacob went to Egypt with all his family.

29Joseph prepared his chariot and went to meet his father. As soon as Joseph saw his father, he hugged his neck and cried there for a long time.

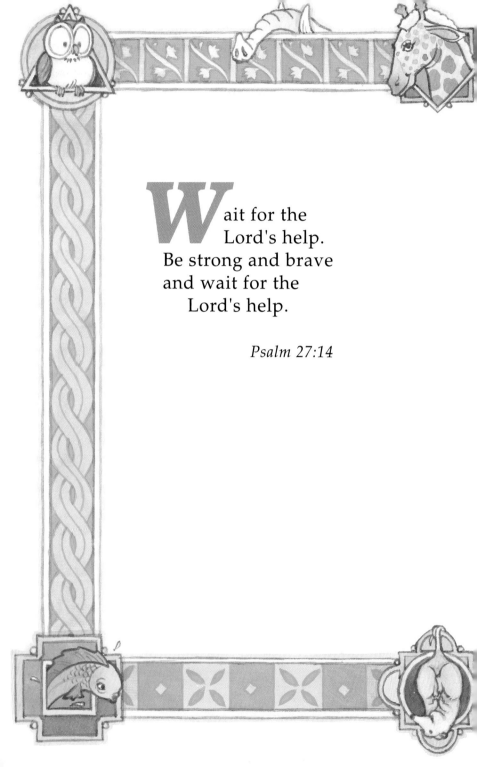

Wait for the
Lord's help.
Be strong and brave
and wait for the
Lord's help.

Psalm 27:14

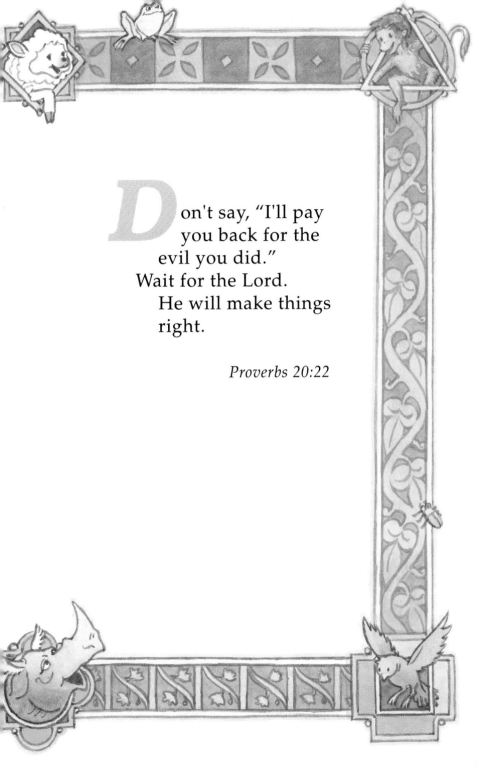

Don't say, "I'll pay you back for the evil you did." Wait for the Lord. He will make things right.

Proverbs 20:22

River Baby

hen a new king began to rule Egypt. ⁹This king said to his people, "The people of Israel are too many! And they are too strong. ¹⁰We must make plans against them. They could fight us and escape from the country!"

¹¹So the Egyptians made life hard for the people of Israel. They put slave masters over the Israelites. The slave masters forced the Israelites to build cities for the king.

¹⁴The Egyptians were not merciful to them in all their hard work.

²² So the king commanded all his people: "Every time a boy is born to the Hebrews, throw him into the Nile River."

(A woman from the family of Levi gave birth to a son. She hid him for three months.)

^{2:3}But after three months, she was not able to hide the baby any longer. So she got a basket and covered it with tar so that it would float. She put the baby in the basket. Then she put the basket among the tall grass at the edge of the Nile River.

⁴The baby's sister stood a short distance away.

⁵Then the daughter of the king of Egypt came to the river. She was going to take a bath. She saw the basket. So she sent her slave girl to get it. ⁶The king's daughter opened the basket and saw the baby boy. He was crying, and she felt sorry for him. She said, "This is one of the Hebrew babies."

⁷Then the baby's sister asked the king's daughter, "Would you like me to find a Hebrew woman to nurse the baby for you?"

⁸The king's daughter said, "Yes." So the girl went and got the baby's own mother.

⁹The king's daughter said, "Take this baby and nurse him for me. I will pay you."

So the woman took her baby and nursed him. ¹⁰After the child had grown older, the king's daughter adopted the baby as her own son. The king's daughter named him Moses, because she had pulled him out of the water.

The Burning Bush

Moses grew and became a man. One day he visited his people, the Hebrews. He saw an Egyptian beating a Hebrew. ¹²So he killed the Egyptian and hid his body in the sand.

¹⁵When the king heard about what Moses had done, he tried to kill Moses. But Moses ran away from the king and went to live in the land of Midian.

¹⁶There was a priest in Midian who had seven daughters. His daughters went to the well to get water for their father's sheep.

¹⁷Some shepherds came and chased the girls away. Then Moses defended the girls and watered their sheep.

¹⁸They went back to their father, Jethro. He asked them, "Why have you come home early today?"

¹⁹The girls answered, "The shepherds chased us away. But an Egyptian defended us. He got water for us and watered our sheep."

²⁰He asked his daughters, "Where is this man? Invite him to eat with us."

²¹Moses agreed to stay with Jethro. He gave his daughter Zipporah to Moses to be his wife.

³:¹One day Moses was taking care of Jethro's sheep. ²The angel of the Lord appeared to Moses in flames of fire coming out of a bush. Moses saw that the bush was on fire, but it was not burning up.

⁴God called to him from the bush,
"Moses, Moses!
⁵"Do not come any closer. Take off your
sandals. You are standing on holy ground.
⁶I am the God of your ancestors.
⁷"I have seen the troubles my people
have suffered in Egypt. ¹⁰So now I am
sending you to the king of Egypt. Go!
Bring my people, the Israelites, out of
Egypt!"

Let My People Go

The king of Egypt did not want to let the Israelites go.
God sent ten terrible disasters on Egypt to make them listen.

During the night the king called for Moses and Aaron. He said to them, "Get up and leave my people. You and your people may do as you have asked. Go and worship the Lord."

³⁷There were about 600,000 men walking. This does not include the women and children.

^{13:17}The king sent the people out of Egypt. ¹⁸God led them through the desert toward the Red Sea.

²¹During the day he went ahead of them in a pillar of cloud. And during the night the Lord was in a pillar of fire to give them light.

^{14:5}The king of Egypt was told that the people of Israel had already left. Then he and his officers changed their minds about them.

¹⁰The Israelites saw the king and his army coming after them. They were very frightened and cried to the Lord for help.

¹⁵Then the Lord said to Moses, ¹⁶"Raise your walking stick and hold it over the sea. The sea will split. Then the people can cross the sea on dry land."

²¹All that night the Lord drove back the sea with a strong east wind. ²²And the Israelites went through the sea on dry land. A wall of water was on both sides.

²³Then all the king's horses, chariots and chariot drivers followed them into the sea. ²⁶Then the Lord told Moses, "Hold your hand over the sea. Then the water will come back over the Egyptians." ²⁷So Moses raised his hand over the sea. And at dawn the water became deep again.

The Egyptians were trying to run from it. But the Lord swept them away into the sea. ²⁸Not one of them survived.

²⁹But the people of Israel crossed the sea on dry land. There was a wall of water on their right and on their left. ³¹And they trusted the Lord.

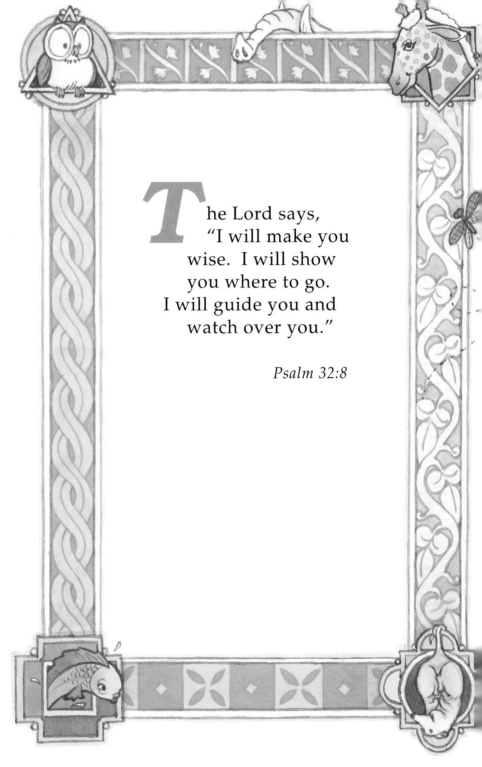

*T*he Lord says,
"I will make you
wise. I will show
you where to go.
I will guide you and
watch over you."

Psalm 32:8

*E*very word of God
can be trusted.
He protects those who
come to him for
safety.

Proverbs 30:5

God Shows Joshua His Power

After Moses died, the Lord said to Joshua: "Just as I was with Moses, so I will be with you.

⁶"Joshua, be strong and brave! You must lead these people so they can take their land. ⁹Don't be afraid. The Lord your God will be with you everywhere you go."

⁴:¹⁰The Lord had commanded Joshua to tell the people what to do. ¹³They went toward the plains of Jericho to go to war.

⁶:¹Now the people of Jericho were afraid because the Israelites were near. So they closed the city gates and guarded them.

No one went into the city. And no one came out.

²The Lord spoke to Joshua. He said, "Look, I have given you Jericho, its king and all its fighting men. ³March around the city with your army one time every day. Do this for six days. ⁴On the seventh day march around the city seven times. On that day tell the priests to blow trumpets as they march.

⁵"When you hear that sound, have all the people give a loud shout. Then the walls of the city will fall. And the people will go straight into the city."

⁸So Joshua finished speaking to the people. Then the seven priests began marching before the Lord. They carried the seven trumpets and blew them as they marched.

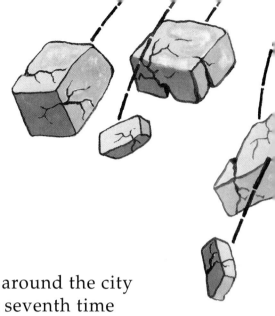

¹⁵They marched around the city
seven times. ¹⁶The seventh time
around, the priests blew their trumpets.
²⁰When the priests blew the trumpets,
the people shouted. At the sound of the
trumpets and the people's shout, the walls
fell. The Israelites defeated that city.
²⁷So the Lord was with Joshua. And
Joshua became famous through all the
land.

^{10:1}The Gibeonites had made a peace agreement with Israel.

⁵Five Amorite kings joined their armies. These armies went to Gibeon, surrounded it and attacked it.

⁶The Gibeonites sent a message to Joshua. The message said: "Don't let us be destroyed. Come quickly and help us!"

⁷So Joshua marched out of Gilgal with his whole army. ⁸The Lord said to Joshua, "Don't be afraid of those armies. I will allow you to defeat them."

⁹Joshua and his army marched all night to Gibeon. So Joshua surprised them when he attacked.

¹¹While they were chasing them, the Lord threw large hailstones on them from the sky. Many of the enemy were killed by the hailstones. More were killed by the hailstones than the Israelites killed with their swords.

¹²Joshua stood before all the people of Israel and said to the Lord: "Sun, stand still over Gibeon." ¹³So the sun stood still until the people defeated their enemies. The sun stopped in the middle of the sky. It waited to go down for a full day. ¹⁴That has never happened at any time before that day or since. Truly the Lord was fighting for Israel!

Samson, the Strong Man

Samson was a man of great strength who had killed many Philistines, Israel's enemies. A woman named Delilah had tried three times to find the secret of Samson's strength so she could sell the secret to his enemies. But each time Samson had fooled her.

elilah said to Samson, "How can you say, 'I love you,' when you don't even trust me? You haven't told me the secret of your great strength." [16]She kept bothering Samson about his secret day after day.

[17]So he told her everything. He said, "I have never had my hair cut. I have been set apart to God since I was born. If someone shaved my head, then I would lose my strength."

[18]Delilah sent a message to the kings of the Philistines. They brought the silver they had promised to give her. [19]Delilah got Samson to go to sleep. He was lying in her lap. Then she called in a man to shave off the seven braids of Samson's hair. And Samson's strength left him.

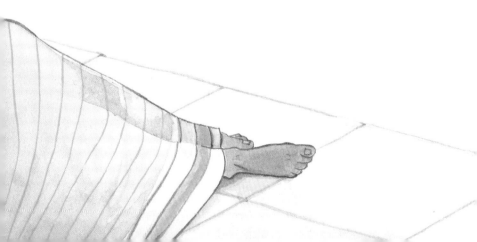

²¹Then the Philistines captured Samson.
They tore out his eyes. They put him in
prison and made him grind grain.

²³The kings of the Philistines gathered to celebrate. They were going to offer a great sacrifice to their god Dagon. They said, "Our god has given us Samson our enemy."

²⁵So they brought Samson from the prison. They made him stand between the pillars of the temple of Dagon.

²⁷Now the temple was full of men and women. All the kings of the Philistines were there. ²⁸Then Samson prayed to the Lord. He said, "Lord God, remember me. God, please give me strength one more time. Let me pay these Philistines back for putting out my two eyes!" ²⁹Then Samson held the two center pillars of the temple. These two pillars supported the whole temple. ³⁰Samson said, "Let me die with these Philistines!" Then he pushed as hard as he could. And the temple fell on the kings and all the people in it. So Samson killed more of the Philistines when he died than when he was alive.

G od is our
protection and
our strength.
He always helps in
times of trouble.

Psalm 46:1

Respect the Lord and refuse to do wrong.
Then your body will be healthy.
And your bones will be strong.

Proverbs 3:7, 8

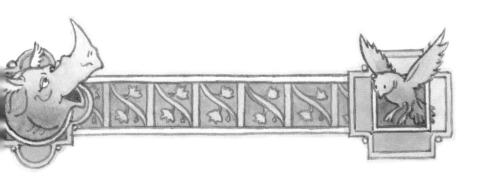

David Fights the Giant

The Philistines gathered their armies for war. ³The Philistines controlled one hill. The Israelites controlled another. The valley was between them.

⁴The Philistines had a champion fighter named Goliath. He was about nine feet four inches tall. ⁵He had a bronze helmet on his head. He wore a coat of armor.

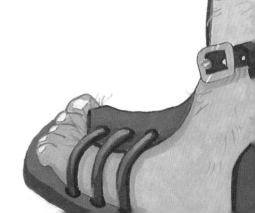

[8]Goliath stood and shouted to the Israelite soldiers, "Choose a man and send him to fight me. [9]If he can fight and kill me, we will become your servants. But if I defeat and kill him, you will become our servants." [11]When Saul and the Israelites heard the Philistine's words, they were very afraid.

[16]The Philistine Goliath came out every morning and evening. He stood before the Israelite army. This continued for 40 days.

(David was a young shepherd, who had brought food for his brothers in Saul's army. He saw that no one would fight Goliath.)

[32]David said to Saul, "I will go and fight this Philistine!"

[33]Saul answered, "You can't go out against this Philistine and fight him. You're only a boy."

³⁴David said to Saul, "I, your servant, have been keeping my father's sheep. When a lion or bear came and took a sheep from the flock, ³⁵I would chase it. ³⁶I have killed both a lion and a bear! Goliath, the Philistine, will be like the lion or bear I killed. He will die because he has stood against the armies of the living God. ³⁷The Lord saved me from a lion and a bear. He will also save me from this Philistine."

Saul said to David, "Go, and may the Lord be with you."

⁴⁰David took his stick in his hand. And he chose five smooth stones from a stream. He put them in his pouch and held his sling in his hand. Then he went to meet Goliath.

⁴²Goliath looked down at David with disgust. ⁴³He said, "Do you think I am a dog, that you come at me with a stick? ⁴⁴Come here. I'll feed your body to the birds of the air and the wild animals!"

⁴⁵But David said to him, "You come to me using a sword, but I come to you in the name of the Lord. You have spoken out against him. ⁴⁶Today the Lord will give you to me. ⁴⁷Everyone gathered here will know the Lord does not need swords or spears to save people. The battle belongs to him! And he will help us defeat all of you."

⁴⁸As Goliath came near to attack him, David ran quickly to meet him. ⁴⁹He took a stone from his pouch. He put it into his sling and slung it. The stone hit the Philistine on his forehead and sank into it. Goliath fell facedown on the ground.

⁵¹David took Goliath's sword out of its holder and killed him.

When the Philistines saw that their champion was dead, they turned and ran.

Elijah Helps a Widow

hab became king of Israel. ³⁰Ahab did many things that the Lord said were wrong. He did more evil than any of the kings before him.

¹⁷:¹Elijah was a prophet. Elijah said to King Ahab, "I serve the Lord. I tell you the truth. No rain or dew will fall during the next few years unless I command it."

²Then the
Lord spoke his
word to Elijah:
³"Leave this place.
Go east and hide. ⁴You may drink from
the brook. And I have commanded ravens
to bring you food there." ⁵So Elijah did
what the Lord told him to do. ⁶The birds
brought Elijah bread and meat every
morning and every evening. And he
drank water from the brook.

⁷The brook dried up because there was no
rain. ⁸Then the Lord spoke to Elijah, ⁹"Go to
Zarephath. Live there. I have commanded
a widow there to take care of you."

¹⁰So Elijah went. When he reached the town gate, he saw a widow there gathering wood for a fire. Elijah asked her, "Would you bring me a drink? ¹¹Please bring me a piece of bread, too."

¹²The woman answered, "I have no bread. I have only a handful of flour in a jar. And I have only a little olive oil in a jug. I came here to gather some wood, take it home, and cook our last meal. My son and I will eat it and then die from hunger."

¹³Elijah said to her, "Go home and cook your food as you have said. But first make a small loaf of bread from the flour you have. Bring it to me. Then cook something for yourself and your son. ¹⁴The Lord said, 'That jar of flour will never become empty. The jug will always have oil in it. This will continue until the day the Lord sends rain to the land.'"

¹⁵So Elijah, the woman and her son had enough food every day.

¹⁷Sometime later the son of the woman became sick. He stopped breathing.

²¹Elijah prayed to the Lord, "Lord my God, let this boy live again!"

²²The Lord answered Elijah's prayer. The boy began breathing again.

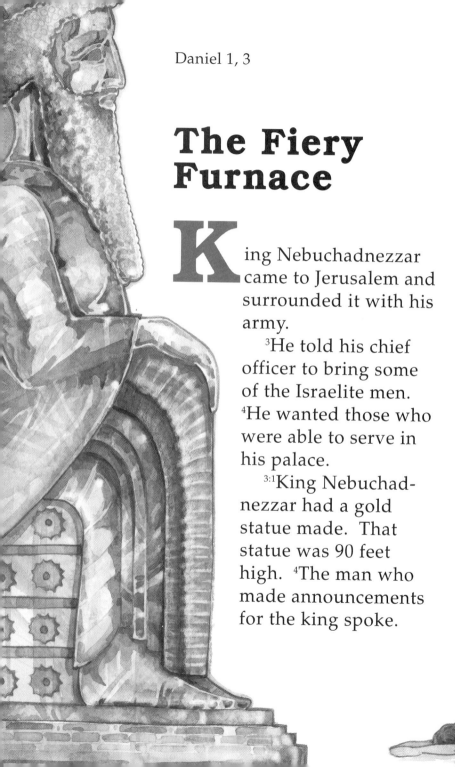

Daniel 1, 3

The Fiery Furnace

King Nebuchadnezzar came to Jerusalem and surrounded it with his army.

³He told his chief officer to bring some of the Israelite men. ⁴He wanted those who were able to serve in his palace.

³:¹King Nebuchadnezzar had a gold statue made. That statue was 90 feet high. ⁴The man who made announcements for the king spoke.

⁶"Everyone must bow down and worship the statue. Anyone who doesn't will be thrown into a blazing furnace." ⁸Some Babylonians came up to the king. They began speaking. ¹²"Our king, some men of Judah did not pay attention to your order. Their names are Shadrach, Meshach and Abednego. They do not worship the gold statue." ¹³Nebuchadnezzar became very angry. He called for those men. ¹⁴"Is it true that you do not serve my gods?"

¹⁶Shadrach, Meshach and Abednego answered the king. They said, "Nebuchadnezzar, we do not need to defend ourselves to you. ¹⁷You can throw us into the blazing furnace. The God we serve is able to save us from the furnace and your power. If he does this, it is good. ¹⁸But even if God does not save us, we want you to know this: We will not worship the gold statue."

²⁰The king told the soldiers to throw them into the furnace. ²³Firmly tied, Shadrach, Meshach and Abednego fell into the blazing furnace.

²⁴Then King Nebuchadnezzar jumped to his feet. He asked the men who advised him, "Didn't we tie up only three men? Didn't we throw them into the fire?

²⁵"Look! I see four men. They are walking around in the fire. They are not tied up, and they are not burned. The fourth man looks like a son of the gods."

²⁶Nebuchadnezzar went to the furnace. He shouted, "Shadrach, Meshach and Abednego, come out!"

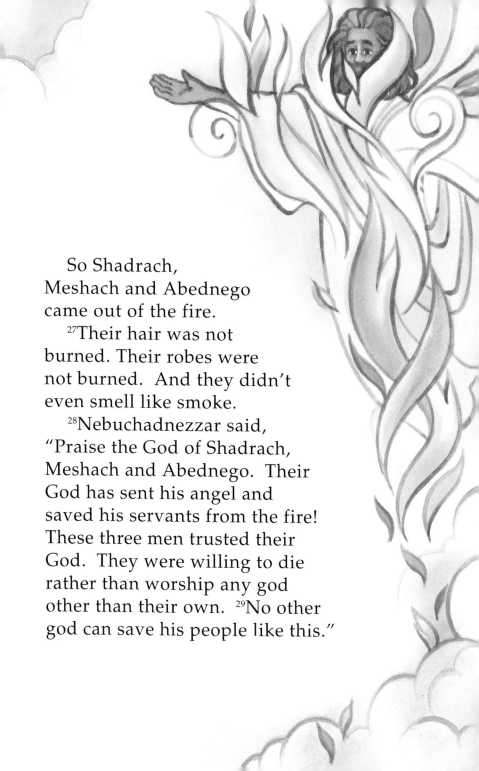

So Shadrach, Meshach and Abednego came out of the fire.

²⁷Their hair was not burned. Their robes were not burned. And they didn't even smell like smoke.

²⁸Nebuchadnezzar said, "Praise the God of Shadrach, Meshach and Abednego. Their God has sent his angel and saved his servants from the fire! These three men trusted their God. They were willing to die rather than worship any god other than their own. ²⁹No other god can save his people like this."

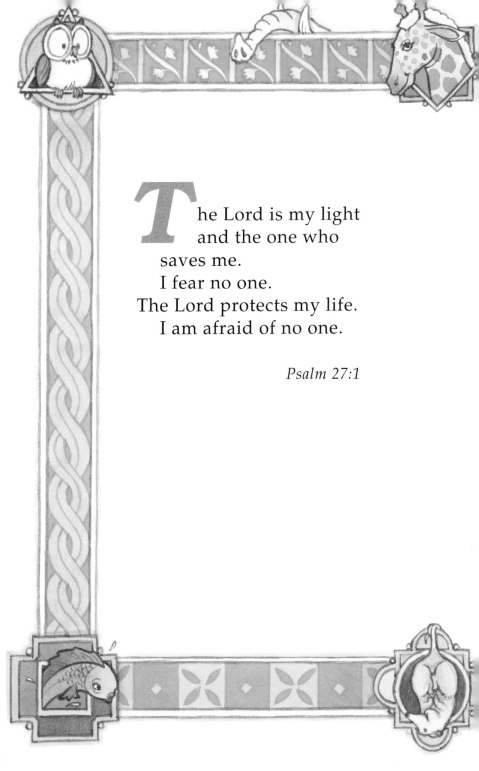

The Lord is my light
and the one who
saves me.
I fear no one.
The Lord protects my life.
I am afraid of no one.

Psalm 27:1

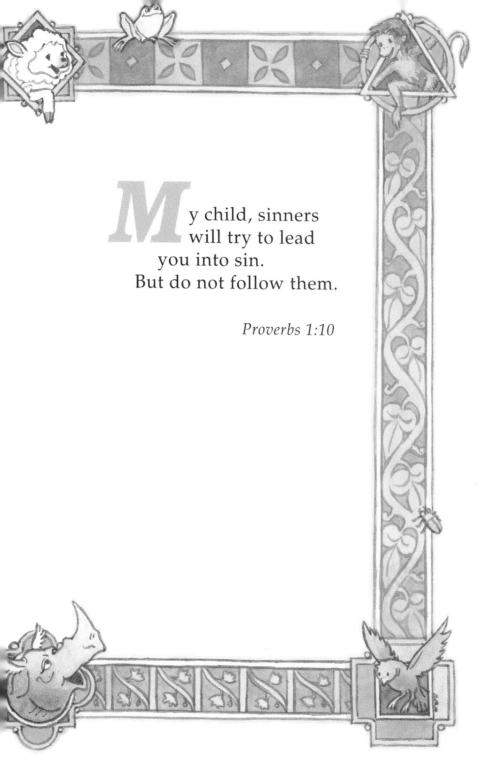

My child, sinners
will try to lead
you into sin.
But do not follow them.

Proverbs 1:10

Daniel 6

Daniel in the Lions' Den

Darius became king of Babylon, over the Jewish captives. Daniel, one of the captives, was picked to help him. The king made a law that said for 30 days people could only pray to the king.

Men spoke to the king. They said, "Daniel is one of the captives from Judah. And he is not paying attention to the law you wrote. Daniel still prays to his God three times every day."

¹⁶They brought Daniel and threw him into the lions' den. The king said to Daniel, "May the God you serve all the time save you!" ¹⁷A big stone was brought. It was put over the opening of the lions' den. Then the king used his signet ring to put his special seal on the rock.

¹⁸Then King Darius went back to his palace. He did not eat that night. And he could not sleep.

¹⁹King Darius got up at dawn. He hurried to the lions' den. ²⁰He called out, "Daniel, servant of the living God! Has your God that you always worship been able to save you from the lions?"

²¹Daniel answered, ²²"My God sent his angel to close the lions' mouths. They have not hurt me, because my God knows I am innocent."

²³So they lifted him out and did not find any injury on him. This was because Daniel had trusted in his God.

Jonah Is Swallowed by a Fish

The Lord spoke to Jonah. ²"Get up, go to the city of Nineveh and preach against it. I see the evil things they do."

³But Jonah got up to run away from the Lord. He found a ship. Jonah paid for the trip and went aboard.

⁴But the Lord sent a great wind on the sea. This wind made the sea very rough.

The ship was in danger of breaking apart. [5]The sailors were afraid. The men began throwing the cargo into the sea. This would make the ship lighter so it would not sink.

But Jonah had gone down into the ship to lie down. He fell fast asleep. [6]The captain of the ship said, "Get up! Pray to your god! Maybe he will save us!"

⁷The men threw lots. The lot showed that the trouble had happened because of Jonah.

¹⁰Then the men were very afraid. They asked Jonah, "What terrible thing did you do?" They knew Jonah was running away from the Lord because Jonah had told them.

¹¹The wind and the waves of the sea were becoming much stronger. So the men said to Jonah, "What should we do to you to make the sea calm down?"

¹²Jonah said to them, "Pick me up, and throw me into the sea."

¹⁵The men picked up Jonah and threw him into the sea. So the sea became calm.

¹⁷The Lord caused a very big fish to swallow Jonah. Jonah was in the stomach of the fish three days and three nights.

²˸¹While Jonah was in the stomach of the fish, he prayed to the Lord his God.

¹⁰Then the Lord spoke to the fish. And the fish spit Jonah out of its stomach onto the dry land.

³˸¹The Lord said, ²"Get up. Go to the great city Nineveh. Preach against it what I tell you."

³So Jonah obeyed the Lord.

⁶The king of Nineveh ⁷made an announcement. ⁸"Everyone must turn away from his evil life."

¹⁰So God changed his mind and did not do what he had warned. He did not punish them.

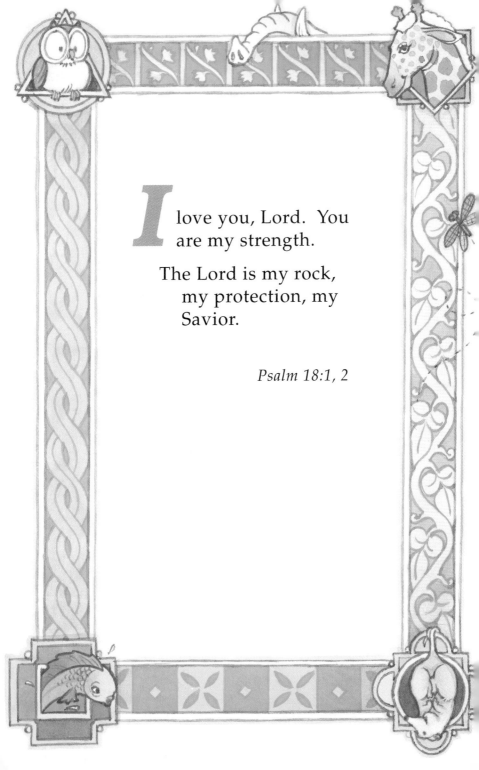

I love you, Lord. You are my strength.

The Lord is my rock, my protection, my Savior.

Psalm 18:1, 2

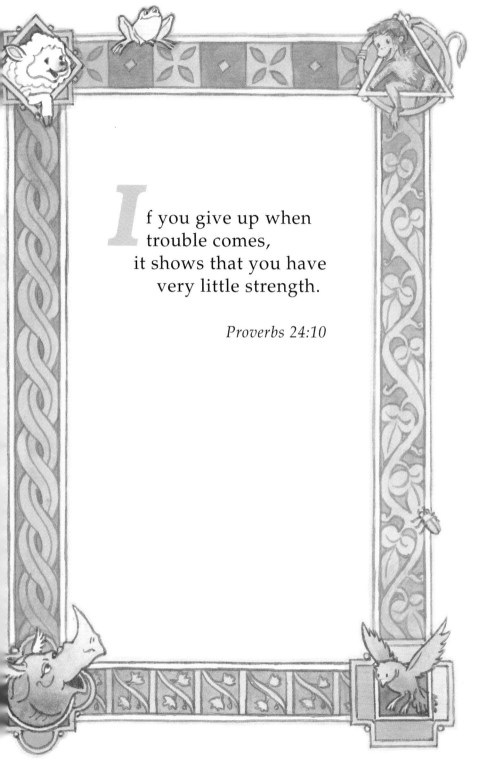

*I*f you give up when
trouble comes,
it shows that you have
very little strength.

Proverbs 24:10

New Testament Stories

and selected

Psalms
and
Proverbs

Jesus Is Born

God sent the angel Gabriel to a virgin who lived in Nazareth, a town in Galilee. She was engaged to marry a man named Joseph from the family of David. Her name was Mary. [28]The angel came to her and said, "Greetings! The Lord has blessed you and is with you.

[30]"Don't be afraid, Mary, because God is pleased with you. You will give birth to a son, and you will name him Jesus. [32]He will be great, and people will call him the Son of the Most High."

[34]Mary said to the angel, "How will this happen? I am a virgin!"

[35]The angel said to Mary, "The Holy Spirit will come upon you, and the power of the Most High will cover you. The baby will be holy. He will be called the Son of God."

[38]Mary said, "I am the servant girl of the Lord. Let this happen to me as you say!"

²:⁶Later, Joseph and Mary were in
Bethlehem, and the time came for her to
have the baby. ⁷She gave birth to her first
son. There were no rooms left in the inn.
So she wrapped the baby with cloths and
laid him in a box where animals are fed.

⁸That night, some shepherds were in the fields nearby, watching their sheep. ⁹An angel of the Lord stood before them.

¹⁰The angel said to them, "Don't be afraid, because I am bringing you some good news. ¹¹Today your Savior was born in David's town. He is Christ, the Lord. ¹²This is how you will know him: You will find a baby wrapped in cloths and lying in a feeding box."

¹³Then a very large group of angels from heaven joined the first angel. All the angels were praising God.

¹⁶So the shepherds went quickly and found Mary and Joseph. ¹⁷They told what the angels had said about this child.

¹⁸Everyone was amazed when they heard what the shepherds said to them. ²⁰Then the shepherds went back to their sheep, praising God and thanking him for everything that they had seen and heard. It was just as the angel had told them.

Wise Men and Danger

J esus was born in the town of Bethlehem when Herod was king. After Jesus was born, some wise men from the east came to Jerusalem. ²They asked, "Where is the baby who was born to be the king of the Jews? We saw his star in the east. We came to worship him."

³When King Herod heard about this new king of the Jews, he was troubled. ⁸He said to them, "When you find him, come tell me. Then I can go worship him too."

⁹The wise men left. They saw the same star they had seen in the east. It went before them until it stopped above the place where the child was. ¹¹They saw him with his mother, Mary. They bowed down and worshiped the child. They opened the gifts they brought for him. ¹²But God warned the wise men in a dream not to go back to Herod. So they went home by a different way.

¹³After they left, an angel of the Lord came to Joseph in a dream and said, "Get up! Take the child and his mother and escape to Egypt. Herod will start looking for the child to kill him."

¹⁴So Joseph left for Egypt during the night with the child and his mother. ¹⁵Joseph stayed in Egypt until Herod died.

¹⁹After Herod died, an angel of the Lord came to Joseph in a dream. ²⁰The angel said, "Get up! Go to Israel. The people who were trying to kill the child are now dead."

²¹So Joseph took the child and his mother and went to Israel. ²³He went to a town called Nazareth and lived there.

*L*ord, I trust you.
I have said,
"You are my God."

Psalm 31:14

W isdom begins
with respect for
the Lord.
And understanding
begins with knowing
God, the Holy One.

Proverbs 9:10

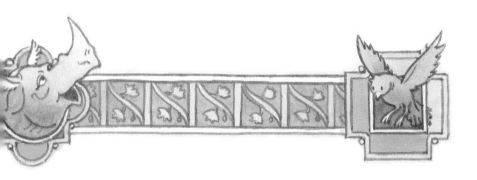

Jesus Grows Up

Every year Jesus' parents went to Jerusalem for the Passover Feast. ⁴²When Jesus was 12 years old, they went to the feast as they always did. ⁴³When the feast days were over, they went home. The boy Jesus stayed behind in Jerusalem, but his parents did not know it. ⁴⁴Joseph and Mary traveled for a whole day.

They thought that Jesus was with them in the group. Then they began to look for him among their family and friends, ⁴⁵but they did not find him. So they went back to Jerusalem to look for him. ⁴⁶After three days they found him. Jesus was sitting in the Temple with the religious teachers, listening to them and asking them questions. ⁴⁷All who heard him were amazed at his understanding and wise answers. ⁴⁸His mother said, "Son, why did you do this to us? Your father and I were very worried about you."

⁴⁹Jesus asked, "Why did you have to look for me? You should have known that I must be where my Father's work is!" ⁵⁰But they did not understand the meaning of what he said.

⁵¹Jesus went with them to Nazareth and obeyed them. ⁵²Jesus continued to learn more and to grow physically. People liked him, and he pleased God.

Jesus Is Baptized

ohn was baptizing people in the desert. They told about the sins they had done. Then they were baptized in the Jordan River. ⁶John wore clothes made from camel's hair and ate locusts and wild honey. ⁷This is what John preached: "There is one coming later who is greater than I. I am not good enough even to kneel down and untie his sandals. ⁸I baptize you with water. But the one who is coming will baptize you with the Holy Spirit."

³:¹⁰The people asked John, "What should we do?"

¹¹John answered, "If you have two shirts, share with the person who does not have one.

If you have food, share that too."
²¹When all the people were being
baptized by John, Jesus also was baptized.
While Jesus was praying, heaven opened
and ²²the Holy Spirit came down on him in
the form of a dove. Then a voice came from
heaven and said, "You are my Son and I
love you. I am very pleased with you."

Jesus Is Tested by the Devil

esus ate nothing for 40 days and nights. After this, he was very hungry. ³The devil came to Jesus to tempt him. The devil said, "If you are the Son of God, tell these rocks to become bread."

⁴Jesus answered, "It is written in the Scriptures, 'A person does not live only by eating bread. But a person lives by everything the Lord says.'"

⁵Then the devil led Jesus to the holy city of Jerusalem. He put Jesus on a very high place of the Temple. ⁶The devil said, "If you are the Son of God, jump off."

⁷Jesus answered him, "It also says in the Scriptures, 'Do not test the Lord your God.'"

⁸Then the devil led Jesus to the top of a very high mountain. He showed Jesus all the kingdoms of the world and all the great things that are in those kingdoms.

[9]The devil said, "If you will bow down and worship me, I will give you all these things."

[10]Jesus said to the devil, "Go away from me, Satan! It is written in the Scriptures, 'You must worship the Lord your God. Serve only him!'"

[11]So the devil left Jesus. And then some angels came to Jesus and helped him.

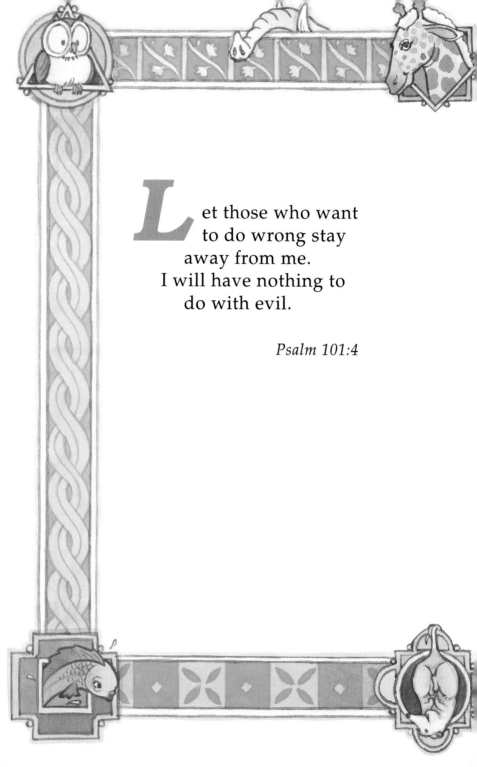

*L*et those who want
to do wrong stay
away from me.
I will have nothing to
do with evil.

Psalm 101:4

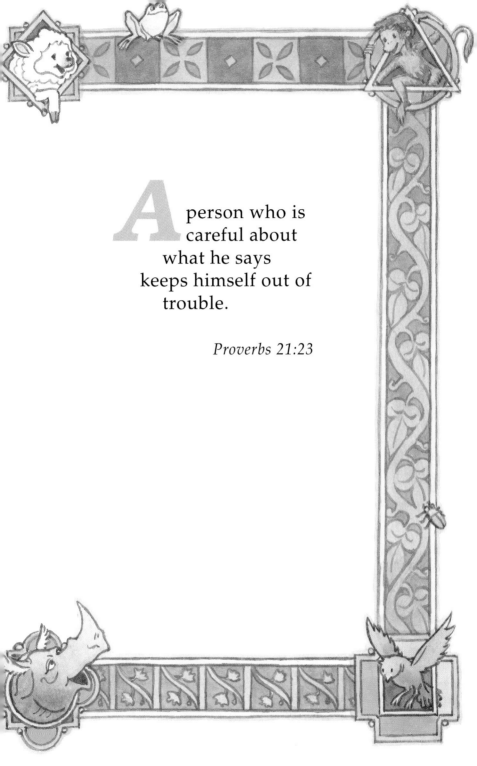

A person who is careful about what he says keeps himself out of trouble.

Proverbs 21:23

Luke 5

A Miracle of Fish

One day Jesus was standing beside Lake Galilee. Many people were pressing all around him. They wanted to hear the word of God. ²Jesus saw two boats at the shore of the lake. ³Jesus got into the one which belonged to Simon. Jesus sat down in the boat and continued to teach the people on the shore.

⁴When Jesus had finished, he said to Simon, "Take the boat into deep water. If you will put your nets in the water, you will catch some fish."

⁵Simon answered, "Master, we worked hard all night trying to catch fish, but we caught nothing. But you say to put the nets in the water; so I will." ⁶And they caught so many fish that the nets began to break! ⁷They called to their friends in the other boat to come and help them. The friends came, and both

boats were
filled so
full that
they were
almost sinking.
⁸The fishermen
were all amazed at
the many fish they
caught.
¹⁰Jesus said to Simon,
"Don't be afraid. From now on
you will be fishermen for men."
¹¹When the men brought
their boats to the shore,
they left everything
and followed
Jesus.

Mark 2

A Man Comes through the Roof

A few days later, Jesus came back home. ²So many people gathered to hear him preach that the house was full. Jesus was teaching them. ³Some people came, bringing a paralyzed man to Jesus. ⁴But they could not get to Jesus because of the crowd. So they went to the roof above Jesus and made a hole in the roof. Then they lowered the mat with the paralyzed man on it. ⁵Jesus saw that these men had great faith. So he said to the paralyzed man, "Young man, your sins are forgiven."

⁶Some of the teachers of the law were sitting there. They saw what Jesus did, and they said, ⁷"Why does this man say things like that? Only God can forgive sins."

⁸At once Jesus knew what these teachers of the law were thinking. So he said to them, ⁹ "Which is easier: to tell this paralyzed man, 'Your sins are forgiven,' or to tell him, 'Stand up. Take your mat and walk'? ¹⁰But I will prove to you that the Son of Man has authority on earth to forgive sins." So Jesus said to the paralyzed man, ¹¹"I tell you, stand up. Take your mat and go home." ¹²Immediately the paralyzed man stood up. He took his mat and walked out while everyone was watching him.

The people were amazed and praised God. They said, "We have never seen anything like this!"

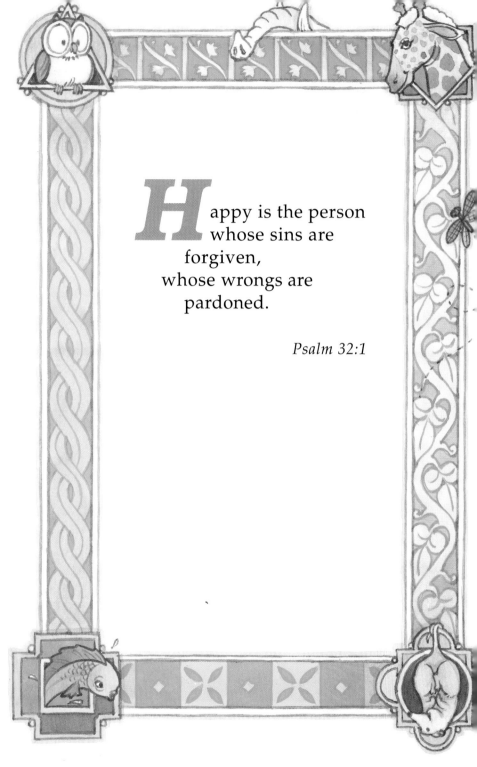

*H*appy is the person whose sins are forgiven, whose wrongs are pardoned.

Psalm 32:1

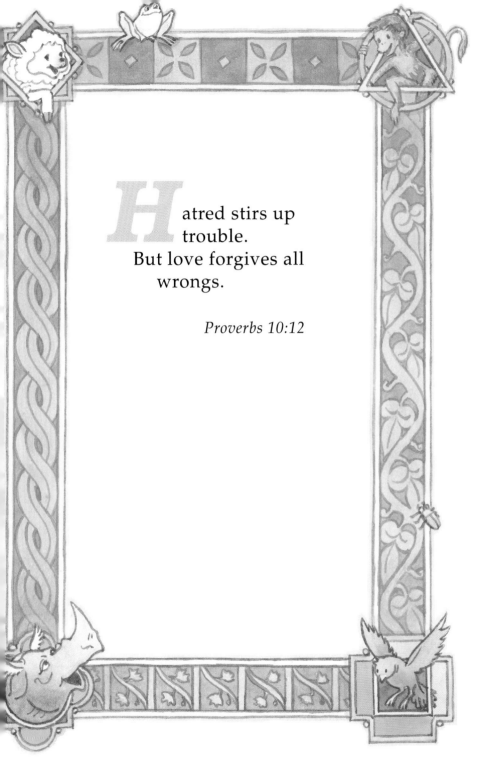

Hatred stirs up trouble.
But love forgives all wrongs.

Proverbs 10:12

Jesus Heals a Boy

One of the king's important officers lived in the city of Capernaum. This man's son was sick. ⁴⁷He went to Jesus and begged him to come and heal his son. His son was almost dead.

⁴⁹The officer said, "Sir, come before my child dies!"

⁵⁰Jesus answered, "Go. Your son will live."

The man believed what Jesus told him and went home. ⁵¹On the way the man's servants came and met him. They told him, "Your son is well."

⁵²The man asked, "What time did my son begin to get well?"

They answered, "It was about one o'clock yesterday when the fever left him."

⁵³The father knew that one o'clock was the exact time that Jesus had said, "Your son will live." So the man and all the people of his house believed in Jesus.

Mark 4

Jesus Calms a Storm

That evening, Jesus said to his followers, "Come with me across the lake." ³⁶They went in the boat that Jesus was already sitting in. ³⁷A very strong wind came up on the lake. The waves began coming over the sides and into the boat. It was almost full of water. ³⁸Jesus was at the back of the boat, sleeping with his head on a pillow. The followers went to him and woke him. They said, "Teacher, do you care about us? We will drown!"

³⁹Jesus stood up and commanded the wind and the waves to stop. He said, "Quiet! Be still!" Then the wind stopped, and the lake became calm. ⁴¹The followers were very afraid and asked each other, "What kind of man is this? Even the wind and the waves obey him!"

The Lord's Prayer

Our Father in heaven, we pray that your name will always be kept holy. ¹⁰We pray that your kingdom will come. We pray that what you want will be done, here on earth as it is in heaven. ¹¹Give us the food we need for each day. ¹²Forgive the sins we have done, just as we have forgiven those who did wrong to us. ¹³Do not cause us to be tested; but save us from the Evil One.' *Amen.*

Matthew 6:9-13

The Golden Rule

Do for other people
what you want
them to do for you.

Luke 6:31

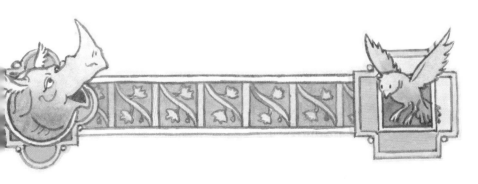

Jesus Feeds 5,000 People

The apostles that Jesus had sent out to preach returned. They gathered around him and told him about all the things they had done and taught. ³¹Crowds of people were coming and going. Jesus and his followers did not even have time to eat. He said to them, "Come with me. We will go to a quiet place to be alone. There we will get some rest."

³²So they went in a boat alone to a place where there were no people. ³³But many people saw them leave and recognized them. So people from all the towns ran to the place where Jesus was going. They got there before Jesus arrived. ³⁴When he landed, he saw a great crowd waiting. Jesus felt sorry for them, because they were like sheep without a shepherd. So he taught them many things.

³⁵It was now late in the day. Jesus' followers came to him and said, "No one lives in this place. And it is already very late. ³⁶Send the people away. They need to go to the farms and towns around here to buy some food to eat."

³⁷But Jesus answered, "You give them food to eat."

They said to him, "We can't buy enough bread to feed all these people! We would all have to work a month to earn enough money to buy that much bread!"

³⁸Jesus asked them, "How many loaves of bread do you have now? Go and see."

When they found out, they came to him and said, "We have five loaves and two fish."

³⁹Then Jesus said to the followers, "Tell all the people to sit in groups on the green grass." ⁴⁰So all the people sat in groups. They sat in groups of 50 or groups of 100. ⁴¹Jesus took the five loaves and two fish. He looked up to heaven and thanked God for the bread.

He divided the bread and gave it to his followers for them to give to the people. Then he divided the two fish among them all. [42]All the people ate and were satisfied. [43]The followers filled 12 baskets with the pieces of bread and fish that were not eaten. [44]There were about 5,000 men there who ate.

Jesus Walks on Water

Jesus made his followers get into the boat. He told them to go ahead of him to the other side of the lake. ²³Jesus went alone into the hills to pray. The boat was already far away on the lake. The boat was having trouble because of the waves and the wind.

²⁵Between three and six o'clock in the morning, Jesus' followers were still in the boat. Jesus came to them walking on water. ²⁶They were afraid. They said, "It's a ghost!" and cried out in fear.

²⁷But Jesus said, "It is I! Don't be afraid."

²⁸Peter said, "Lord, if that is really you, then tell me to come to you on the water."

²⁹Jesus said, "Come." Peter left the boat and walked on the water to Jesus. ³⁰But when Peter saw the wind and the waves, he became afraid and began to sink. He shouted, "Lord, save me!"

³¹Then Jesus reached out his hand and caught Peter. Jesus said, "Your faith is small. Why did you doubt?"

³²After Peter and Jesus were in the boat, the wind became calm. Those who were in the boat said, "Truly you are the Son of God!"

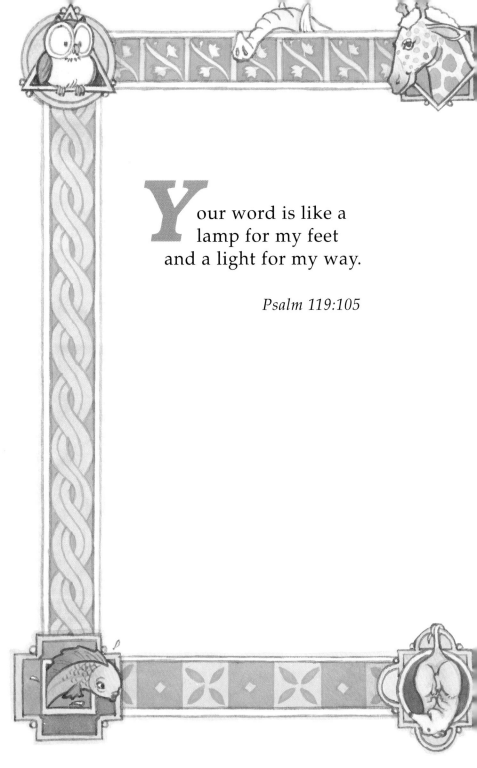

Your word is like a lamp for my feet and a light for my way.

Psalm 119:105

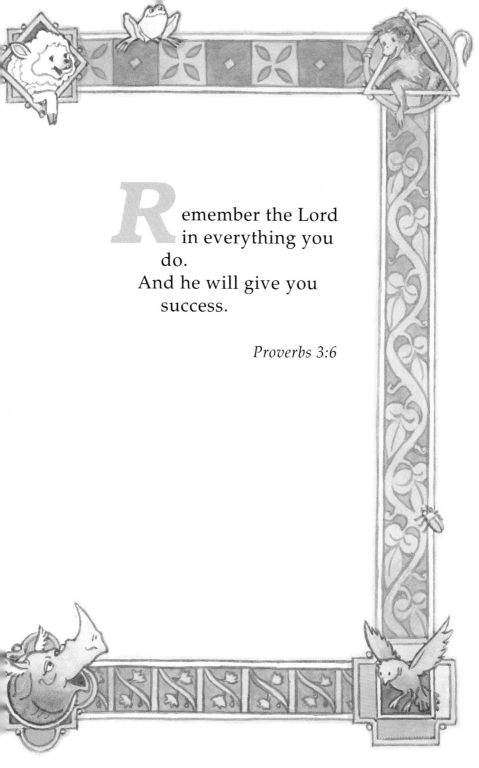

Remember the Lord in everything you do.
And he will give you success.

Proverbs 3:6

Luke 10

Who is My Neighbor?

J esus said, "A man was going down the road. Some robbers attacked him. They tore off his clothes and beat him. Then they left him lying there, almost dead. [31]A Jewish priest was going down the road. When the priest saw the man, he walked by on the other side of the road. [32]Next, a Levite came there. Then he walked by on the other side of the road.

³³Then a Samaritan came to where the hurt man was lying. ³⁴The Samaritan went to him and poured olive oil and wine on his wounds and bandaged them. He put the hurt man on his own donkey and took him to an inn.

³⁵"The Samaritan brought out two silver coins and gave them to the innkeeper. The Samaritan said, 'Take care of this man. If you spend more money on him, I will pay it back to you when I come again.'"

³⁶Then Jesus said, "Which one of these three men do you think was a neighbor to the man who was attacked by the robbers?"

³⁷The teacher of the law answered, "The one who helped him."

Jesus said to him, "Then go and do the same thing he did!"

Mark 12

The Widow's Gift

Jesus sat near the Temple money box where people put their gifts. He watched the people put in their money. Many rich people gave large sums of money. ⁴²Then a poor widow came and gave two very small copper coins. These coins were not worth even a penny.

⁴³Jesus called his followers to him. He said, "I tell you the truth. This poor widow gave only two small coins. But she really gave more than all those rich people. ⁴⁴The rich have plenty; they gave only what they did not need. This woman is very poor. But she gave all she had. And she needed that money to help her live."

A Blind Man Sees

As Jesus was leaving Jericho with his followers and a large crowd, a blind beggar named Bartimaeus was sitting by the road. ⁴⁷He heard that Jesus from Nazareth was walking by. The blind man cried out, "Jesus, Son of David, please help me!"

⁵¹Jesus asked him, "What do you want me to do for you?"

The blind man answered, "Teacher, I want to see again."

⁵²Jesus said, "Go. You are healed because you believed." At once the man was able to see again, and he followed Jesus on the road.

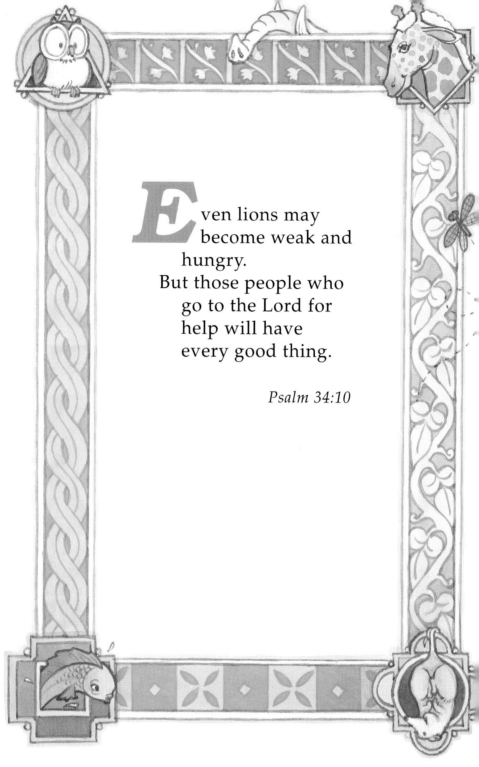

*E*ven lions may become weak and hungry.
But those people who go to the Lord for help will have every good thing.

Psalm 34:10

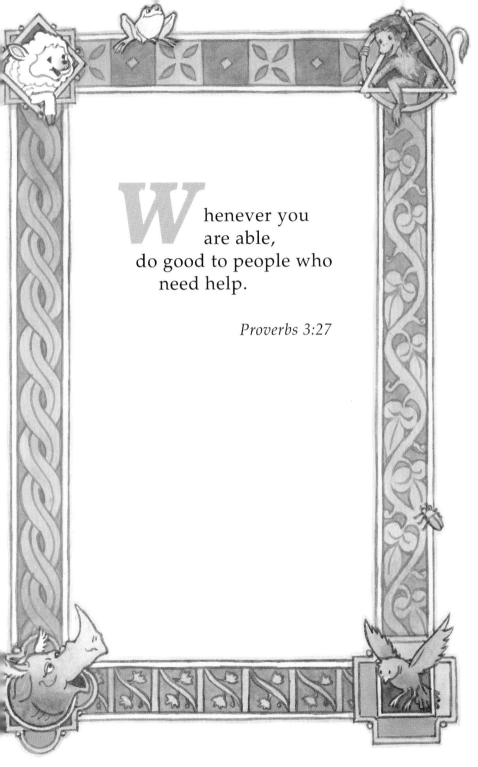

Whenever you
are able,
do good to people who
need help.

Proverbs 3:27

Judas' Evil Plan

The leading priests and older Jewish leaders had a meeting at the palace of the high priest. The high priest's name was Caiaphas. ⁴At the meeting, they planned to set a trap to arrest Jesus and kill him.

¹⁴Then 1 of the 12 followers went to talk to the leading priests. This was the follower named Judas Iscariot. ¹⁵He said, "I will give Jesus to you. What will you pay me for doing this?" The priests gave Judas 30 silver coins. ¹⁶After that, Judas waited for the best time to give Jesus to the priests.

¹³:²Jesus and his followers were at the evening meal.

²¹Jesus said, "One of you will turn against me.

²⁶"I will dip this bread into the dish. The man I give it to is the man who will turn against me." So Jesus took a piece of bread and gave it to Judas. ²⁷Jesus said to Judas, "The thing that you will do—do it quickly!"

³⁰Judas accepted the bread Jesus gave him and immediately went out. It was night.

³¹When Judas was gone, ³³Jesus said, "My children, I will be with you only a little longer. Where I am going you cannot come.

³⁴"I give you a new command: Love each other. You must love each other as I have loved you. ³⁵People will know that you are my followers if you love each other."

³²Jesus and his followers went to a place called Gethsemane. He said to his followers, "Sit here while I pray. ³⁴My heart is breaking with sadness."

³⁵Jesus walked a little farther away from them. ³⁶He prayed, "Father! You can do all things. Let me not have this cup of suffering. But do what you want, not what I want."

³⁷Then Jesus went back to his followers. He found them asleep.

⁴¹After Jesus prayed a third time, he said to them, "The time has come for the Son of Man to be given to sinful people. ⁴²Get up! We must go. Here comes the man who has turned against me."

¹⁸:²Judas knew where this place was, because Jesus met there often with his followers. ³Judas led a group of soldiers to the garden. They were carrying torches, lanterns, and weapons.

⁴Jesus knew everything that would happen to him. Jesus went out and asked, "Who is it you are looking for?"

The men answered, "Jesus from Nazareth."

⁸Jesus said, "I told you that I am he. So if you are looking for me, then let these other men go."

¹⁰Simon Peter had a sword.
He took out the sword and
struck the servant of the
high priest, cutting off
his right ear. ¹¹Jesus said
to Peter, "Put your
sword back."
¹²Then the soldiers with
their commander and the
Jewish guards arrested Jesus.

No one who trusts
you will be
disgraced.
But those who sin
without excuse
will be disgraced.

Psalm 25:3

A person who
quickly gets
angry causes trouble.
But a person who
controls his temper
stops a quarrel.

Proverbs 15:18

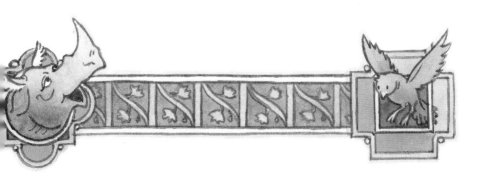

Jesus Dies on a Cross

The people who arrested Jesus led him to the house of the high priest. [55]The leading priests tried to find something that Jesus had done wrong so they could kill him. But the council could find no proof against him.

[61]The high priest asked Jesus: "Are you the Christ, the Son of the blessed God?"

[62]Jesus answered, "I am."

[63]When the high priest heard this, he was very angry and said, [64]"You all heard him say these things against God. What do you think?"

They all said that Jesus was guilty and should be killed.

[23:1]The whole group stood up and led Jesus to Pilate.

[3]Pilate asked Jesus, "Are you the king of the Jews?"

Jesus answered, "Yes."

[7]Pilate sent Jesus to Herod. [9]Herod asked Jesus many questions, but Jesus said nothing. [11]Herod and his soldiers made fun of Jesus. They dressed him in a kingly robe and then sent him back to Pilate.

[13]Pilate called all the people together with the leading priests and Jewish leaders.

¹⁴He said, "You brought this man to me. You said that he was making trouble among the people. He has done nothing for which he should die. ¹⁶So, after I punish him, I will let him go free."

¹⁸But all the people shouted, "Kill him!"

²⁴Pilate decided to give them what they wanted. ²⁵Pilate gave Jesus to them to be killed.

²⁶The soldiers led Jesus away. The soldiers forced Simon to carry Jesus' cross and walk behind him.

There were also two criminals led out with Jesus to be killed. ³³The soldiers nailed Jesus to his cross. They nailed the criminals to their crosses, one beside Jesus on the right and the other beside Jesus on the left.

³⁴Jesus said, "Father, forgive them. They don't know what they are doing."

⁴⁴It was about noon, and the whole land became dark until three o'clock in the afternoon. ⁴⁵There was no sun! ⁴⁶Jesus cried out in a loud voice, "Father, I give you my life." After Jesus said this, he died.

⁴⁸Many people had gathered there. When they saw what happened, they returned home. They were so sad. ⁴⁹Close friends of Jesus were there. Some were women. They all stood far away from the cross and watched.

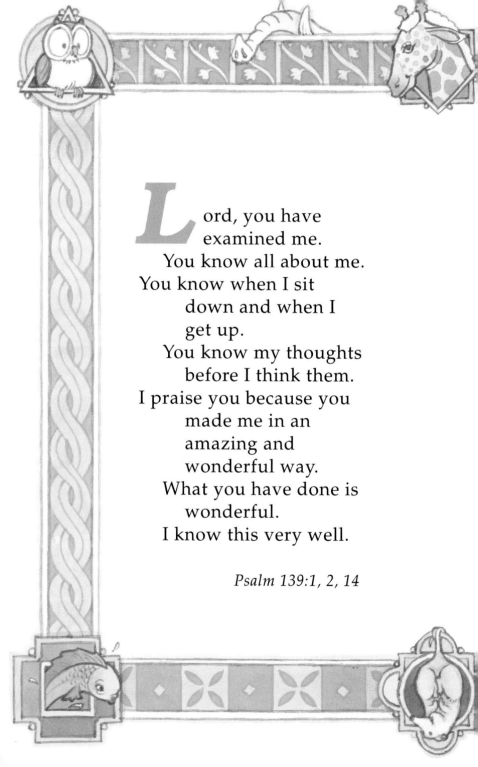

*L*ord, you have
examined me.
You know all about me.
You know when I sit
down and when I
get up.
You know my thoughts
before I think them.
I praise you because you
made me in an
amazing and
wonderful way.
What you have done is
wonderful.
I know this very well.

Psalm 139:1, 2, 14

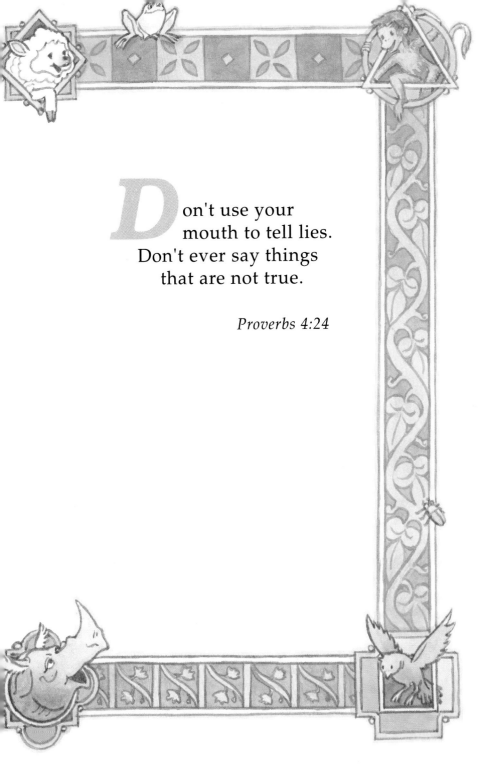

Don't use your
mouth to tell lies.
Don't ever say things
that are not true.

Proverbs 4:24

Jesus Lives Again!

The first day of the week at dawn, Mary Magdalene and another woman named Mary went to the tomb. ²There was a strong earthquake. An angel of the Lord rolled the stone away from the entrance. Then he sat on the stone. ³He was shining as bright as lightning. His clothes were white as snow. ⁴The soldiers guarding the tomb were very frightened. ⁵The angel said to the women, "Don't be afraid. I know that you are looking for Jesus.

⁶He is not here.
He has risen from
death as he said he
would. ⁷Go tell his followers."
    ⁸The women left the tomb quickly.
⁹Suddenly, Jesus met them and said,
"Greetings." The women came up to
Jesus, took hold of his feet, and worshiped
him. ¹⁰Then Jesus said to them, "Don't be
afraid. Go and tell my brothers to go on
to Galilee. They will see me there."

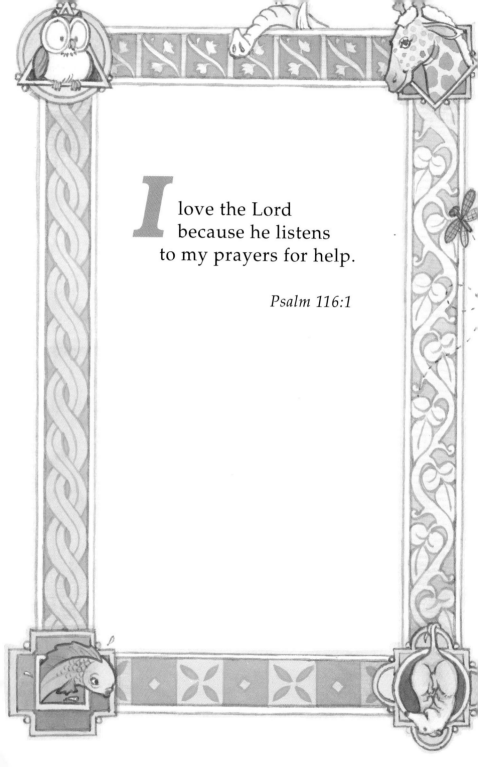

I love the Lord
because he listens
to my prayers for help.

Psalm 116:1

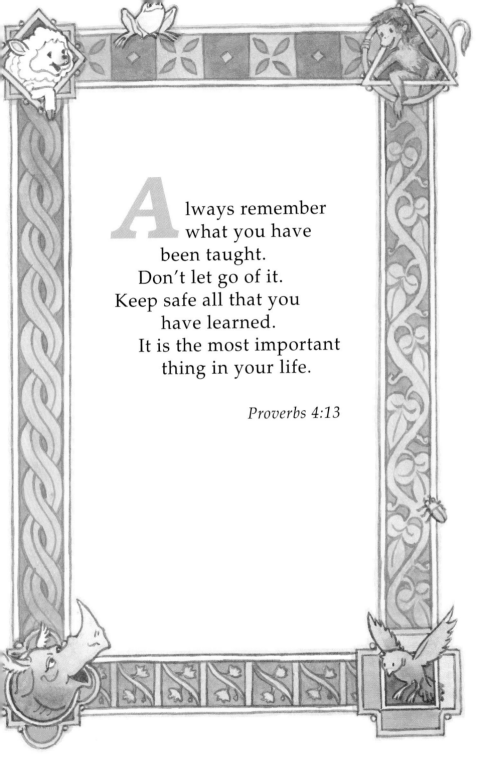

Always remember
what you have
been taught.
Don't let go of it.
Keep safe all that you
have learned.
It is the most important
thing in your life.

Proverbs 4:13

Jesus Appears to Thomas

That evening the followers were together. The doors were locked, because they were afraid. Jesus came and stood among them. He said, "Peace be with you!"

²⁰He showed them his hands and his side. The followers were very happy when they saw the Lord.

²⁴Thomas was not with the followers when Jesus came. ²⁵The other followers told Thomas, "We saw the Lord."

But Thomas said, "I will not believe it until I see the nail marks in his hands. I will not believe until I put my finger where the nails were and put my hand into his side."

²⁶A week later the followers were in the house again. Thomas was with them. The doors were locked, but Jesus came in and stood among them. He said, "Peace be with you!" ²⁷Then he said to Thomas, "Put your finger here. Look at my hands. Put your hand here in my side. Stop doubting and believe."

²⁸Thomas said, "My Lord and my God!"

²⁹Then Jesus told him, "You believe because you see me. Those who believe without seeing me will be truly happy."

Jesus Returns to Heaven

After his death, he showed himself to them and proved in many ways that he was alive. The apostles saw Jesus during the 40 days after he was raised from death.

He said, [8]"You will be my witnesses in every part of the world." [9]After he said this, as they were watching, he was lifted up. A cloud hid him from their sight.

¹⁰As he was going, they were looking into the sky. Suddenly, two men wearing white clothes stood beside them. ¹¹They said, "Men of Galilee, why are you standing here looking into the sky? You saw Jesus taken away from you into heaven. He will come back in the same way you saw him go."

The Lord is my shepherd. I have everything I need. He gives me rest in green pastures. He leads me to calm water. He gives me new strength. For the good of his name, he leads me on paths that are right. Even if I walk through a very dark valley, I will not be afraid because you are with me. Your rod and your walking stick comfort me.

You prepare a meal for me in front of my enemies. You pour oil on my head. You give me more than I can hold. Surely your goodness and love will be with me all my life. And I will live in the house of the Lord forever.

Psalm 23

Reading Chart

When you have read a story or psalm or proverb all on your own, put a checkmark and the date next to it. Soon you will have read the whole book! Then you can go back and read your favorite stories and verses again and again.

Old Testament Stories and Selected Psalms and Proverbs

On this day I read it myself

_____	❏ God Creates the World
_____	❏ The Snake's Trick
_____	❏ Noah's Adventure
_____	❏ Psalm 25:4
_____	❏ Proverbs 1:8–9
_____	❏ Joseph in the Well
_____	❏ Joseph Rules Egypt
_____	❏ Psalm 27:14
_____	❏ Proverbs 20:22
_____	❏ River Baby
_____	❏ The Burning Bush
_____	❏ Let My People Go
_____	❏ Psalm 32:8
_____	❏ Proverbs 30:5
_____	❏ God Shows Joshua His Power
_____	❏ Samson, the Strong Man
_____	❏ Psalm 46:1
_____	❏ Proverbs 3:7–8
_____	❏ David Fights the Giant
_____	❏ Elijah Helps a Widow
_____	❏ The Fiery Furnace
_____	❏ Psalm 27:1
_____	❏ Proverbs 1:10
_____	❏ Daniel in the Lions' Den
_____	❏ Jonah Is Swallowed by a Fish
_____	❏ Psalm 18:1–2
_____	❏ Proverbs 24:10